The Evolution of Mainframes: A Journey Through Time

Mainframes

Isaac Nangan

Published by Isaac Nangan, 2024.

THE EVOLUTION OF MAINFRAMES: A JOURNEY THROUGH TIME

First edition. April 9, 2024.

ISBN: 978-9815194494

Written by Isaac Nangan.

Table of Contents

.... 1
Preface 2
Prologue 4
Introduction 6
Setting the Stage: The Dawn of the Computing Era 8
The Purpose and Scope of This Journey 10
The Evolution of Mainframes: An Overview 12
Chapter 1: The Birth of Mainframes 15
The First Giants: Early Computers and Their Limitations 18
Technological Breakthroughs: Vacuum Tubes to Transistors 21
The Mainframe in Society: Early Adopters and Impact 24
Chapter 2: The Golden Age of Mainframes 27
The Rise of Business Computing 30
Mainframe Architecture: Design and Development 33
Mainframes and the Public: Accessibility and Influence 36
Chapter 3: The Changing Landscape 39
The Advent of Personal Computers: A Shift in the Market 42
Mainframes vs. Minicomputers: A New Competition 45
Adapting to Change: Mainframe Evolution in the PC Era 48
Chapter 4: The Era of Connectivity 51
Networking and the Internet: A New Role for Mainframes 54
Mainframes in the Digital Age: Powering the Web 57
Security and Reliability: The Unseen Backbone 59
Chapter 5: The Modern Mainframe 62
Innovations and Current Technologies in Mainframe Computing 65
Mainframes in the Cloud Era: New Challenges and Opportunities 68
The Future of Mainframes: Predictions and Possibilities 71
Chapter 6: Mainframes in Culture and Society 74
Mainframes in Media: Perception vs. Reality 76

The Educational Impact: Teaching Mainframe Technologies.......78
The Legacy of Mainframes: Shaping the Computing World 80
Conclusion...83
Reflecting on the Journey: The Continuous Evolution of Mainframes 85
The Role of Mainframes in the Future of Technology 87
Final Thoughts: The Enduring Legacy of Mainframe Computing...89
Epilogue...91
Appendix A: Glossary of Mainframe Terminology 93
Appendix B: Timeline of Mainframe Development 95
Appendix C: Interviews with Mainframe Experts and Historians 98

To Coleen, Sky and Neo. You are my life! You are my inspirations!

The Evolution of Mainframes: A Journey Through Time

Isaac Nangan

Preface

In the annals of computing history, the mainframe stands as a towering testament to human ingenuity, a relentless pursuit of technological advancement, and the indomitable spirit of innovation. This book, "The Evolution of Mainframes: A Journey Through Time," is an homage to the remarkable journey of mainframe computers - from their colossal, room-filling infancy to the sleek, powerful engines of computation they are today.

When embarking on this journey, one cannot help but be in awe of how these technological behemoths have not only survived but thrived, adapting to the relentless tides of technological change. Mainframes have been the silent, steadfast giants upon which the pillars of governments, corporations, and institutions have rested. Yet, in popular culture, they are often overshadowed by their more glamorous counterparts - the personal computers and smartphones. This book aims to shine a light on these unsung heroes of the digital age.

In these pages, readers will discover a narrative that is both rich in history and vibrant with stories of innovation and ingenuity. The book doesn't merely recount the technical advancements and architectural revolutions in mainframe technology; it delves into the societal, economic, and cultural impacts that have been intricately woven into the fabric of this evolution.

The journey of the mainframe is not just a tale of hardware and software. It is a story of challenges and triumphs, of visionaries who saw beyond the horizon, and of unassuming engineers who quietly shaped the digital world. It's about the relentless human quest for faster, more efficient, and more secure ways of processing information.

As you turn these pages, I invite you to join me in exploring the labyrinthine corridors of computing history. Whether you are a seasoned computer historian, a student of technology, an industry professional, or simply a curious mind attracted to the saga of human progress, there is something in this journey for you. This book is not just about understanding where we have been; it is about gaining insights into where we might be headed.

In writing this book, I have endeavored to make the complex world of mainframe computing accessible and engaging. My hope is that by the end of this journey, you will not only have gained a deeper understanding of mainframes and their place in the computing pantheon but also developed an appreciation for the remarkable journey of technological evolution they represent.

Welcome to "The Evolution of Mainframes: A Journey Through Time." Let the journey begin.

Prologue

In a world where the rapid pace of technological advancement often leaves yesterday's marvels gathering dust in the shadow of today's innovations, there exists a technological dynasty that has not only endured but has continually evolved and flourished. This is the world of mainframe computers, the silent giants that have been the backbone of industries and governments for over half a century.

As we stand at the threshold of an era dominated by cloud computing, artificial intelligence, and the Internet of Things, it might seem anachronistic to turn our gaze to these behemoths of the past. Yet, to understand the present and to anticipate the future of computing, one must journey through the rich tapestry of the mainframe's history.

This prologue sets the stage for a story that is as much about remarkable machines as it is about the people who created them, the organizations that were built around them, and the societal changes they precipitated. From their inception, mainframes were more than just pieces of technology; they were harbingers of a new age, catalysts of modern society, and architects of a digital world we now take for granted.

In the ensuing chapters, we will explore the genesis of the mainframe in the post-war era, a time when the world, emerging from the chaos of conflict, was ripe for a technological revolution. We will see how these machines evolved from cumbersome, room-sized calculators to the sleek, powerhouse servers that quietly manage the data of millions today.

The narrative will take us through various technological epochs - from the age of punch cards and vacuum tubes to the era of silicon and cyber-security. We will witness the rise and fall of industry titans, the unsung heroes of the computing saga, and the relentless pursuit of innovation that drove the mainframe's evolution.

But this is not just a tale of circuits and code. It's a story of how technology can transform societies, redefine economies, and alter the course of human history. As you read through the chapters of this book, you will encounter stories of competition and collaboration, challenges and triumphs, and a relentless quest to push the boundaries of what is possible.

The mainframe's journey is far from over. As we look to the future, we find these machines at the heart of some of the most advanced technologies today, from managing complex financial transactions to harnessing the power of big data and artificial intelligence.

In this prologue, we invite you to step into the world of mainframes - a world that, despite its profound influence on our lives, remains largely hidden and uncelebrated. Join us on this journey through time, and discover the enduring legacy of one of the most influential technologies in human history.

Introduction

Setting the Stage: The Dawn of the Computing Era

As we embark on this exploration of mainframes, it's essential to first set the stage with the dawn of the computing era. This era did not start with a singular invention or moment but was a culmination of years of mathematical and engineering breakthroughs. From Charles Babbage's analytical engine in the 19th century to the code-breaking machines of World War II, the foundation for modern computing was laid through a series of innovations. Each of these developments brought us closer to the creation of the first mainframes – machines that would revolutionize how we process information.

The post-World War II period marked a significant turning point. Society was primed for transformation, and technology was poised to lead the charge. The invention of the transistor and the development of electronic circuits opened doors to possibilities that were previously unattainable. It was in this fertile ground that the seeds of the mainframe computer were sown, promising to bring unprecedented computational power to the fingertips of governments and businesses.

The Purpose and Scope of This Journey

This book aims to chronicle the journey of mainframe computers from their inception to their current state, delving into the technological advancements, the changes they brought to society, and their enduring legacy. The purpose of this journey is twofold. Firstly, to provide a comprehensive history of mainframe technology, tracing its evolution through various technological and social landscapes. Secondly, to offer insights into how this evolution has shaped and been shaped by the broader context of computing history.

Throughout the book, we'll explore the technological marvels of mainframes, the challenges they overcame, and the opportunities they created. We will look at the key figures and events that shaped their development and examine the impact of mainframes on business practices, governmental operations, and societal norms.

The Evolution of Mainframes: An Overview

Mainframes began as hulking machines that filled entire rooms, yet were less powerful than today's simplest handheld devices. Their evolution is a story of rapid technological progress and adaptation. This story is marked by milestones like the transition from vacuum tubes to transistors, then to integrated circuits, and eventually to the microprocessors we know today. Each of these shifts brought about changes in mainframe architecture, functionality, and application.

As we progress through this history, we'll see how mainframes, often perceived as relics of the past, have continually reinvented themselves to stay relevant. Their journey is interwoven with the development of programming languages, the rise of networking, and the emergence of cybersecurity concerns. In the modern era, we find mainframes at the heart of cloud computing and big data analytics, still performing critical tasks that require their unique combination of reliability, security, and processing power.

In summary, this introduction paves the way for a detailed exploration of the world of mainframes. From their early days to their current, often unnoticed, role in modern computing, we are about to embark on a journey through time, celebrating an often-overlooked but vital piece of technological history. Welcome to the fascinating world of mainframes.

Setting the Stage: The Dawn of the Computing Era

The dawn of the computing era was not marked by a single invention but was rather a crescendo of cumulative breakthroughs in mathematics and engineering. This era can be traced back to the early 19th century with the visionary work of Charles Babbage. Babbage's designs for the Difference Engine and the more complex Analytical Engine laid the foundational concepts of programmable computing. Although Babbage never completed these machines, his ideas were far ahead of their time, introducing concepts like the stored program and the use of punch cards for instructions.

Fast forward to the early 20th century, when the invention of the vacuum tube laid the groundwork for electronic computation. Vacuum tubes, which could amplify signals and act as switches, were integral to the development of early computers. During World War II, the exigencies of war catalyzed significant advancements in computing. Machines like the British Colossus and the American ENIAC were developed for code-breaking and ballistic calculations. These machines, though primitive by today's standards, were revolutionary. They demonstrated the potential of electronic computing to process information at unprecedented speeds.

However, it was in the post-World War II era that the stage was truly set for the advent of mainframes. Society, having witnessed the transformative power of technology during the war, was ripe for a new era of innovation. Two critical developments during this period played pivotal roles. First, the invention of the transistor in 1947 by Bell Labs marked a significant advancement. Transistors were smaller, more reliable, and more energy-efficient than vacuum tubes, paving the way for more complex and compact computers.

Secondly, the development of electronic circuits, especially the printed circuit board, allowed for more components to be integrated into smaller spaces. This integration was crucial for the development of computers that could handle more complex operations and store more data.

Into this fertile technological landscape, the concept of the mainframe computer was introduced. Unlike their predecessors, which were often custom-built for specific tasks, mainframes were designed to be more versatile and powerful. They were conceived to handle large-scale computations required by governments and growing businesses, from census data processing to complex scientific calculations.

Mainframes marked a shift from mechanical to electronic computing, harnessing the power of transistors and circuitry to deliver capabilities that were previously unthinkable. They represented not just a technological leap but also a new vision of the future – a world where complex data could be processed rapidly and efficiently, opening doors to new possibilities in business, science, and government administration.

In summary, the dawn of the computing era was a tapestry of innovations, visions, and necessities, woven together over centuries. The stage was set not by a single invention but by a series of advancements that gradually built the foundation for the mainframes. These machines would not only revolutionize how we process information but also lay the groundwork for the digital world we live in today.

The Purpose and Scope of This Journey

The journey through the history of mainframe computers is a voyage across time, technology, and society. The purpose of this exploration is twofold. Firstly, it aims to chronicle a comprehensive history of mainframe technology, tracing its lineage from the earliest calculating machines to the sophisticated systems of today. This exploration is not just about understanding the hardware but also about appreciating the software developments, the design philosophies, and the engineering milestones that have defined the mainframe's evolution.

Secondly, this journey seeks to offer insights into how the evolution of mainframes has both shaped and been shaped by the broader context of computing history. This aspect delves into the symbiotic relationship between mainframe development and the wider technological and social landscape. By understanding this relationship, we can appreciate how mainframes have been both a driver and a reflection of changes in computing practices, business strategies, and societal norms.

Throughout this book, the focus will be on exploring the technological marvels of mainframes, highlighting not just the triumphs but also the significant challenges they overcame. These challenges often spurred innovations that went beyond the realm of mainframes, influencing the entire field of computing. We will delve into the architectural evolution of mainframes, the shift in processing paradigms, and the breakthroughs in storage and networking technologies that have been integral to their development.

Moreover, the narrative will spotlight key figures and events that played pivotal roles in the development of mainframes. From visionary engineers and developers to influential corporate leaders, their stories are crucial in understanding the trajectory of mainframe technology. This exploration will also shed light on lesser-known contributors whose innovations were critical in shaping the mainframe landscape.

In examining the impact of mainframes on business and government, the book will explore how these machines revolutionized data processing, transaction handling, and information management. Mainframes ushered in a new era in sectors such as banking, insurance, and government administration, enabling these institutions to handle large volumes of data with unprecedented speed and reliability.

Furthermore, the social implications of mainframes are an integral part of this story. The book will discuss how mainframes have influenced societal norms and expectations around data privacy, cybersecurity, and even the concept of work in a digital age. It will also touch upon the cultural representation of mainframes, examining how they have been perceived and portrayed in media and popular culture.

In summary, the purpose and scope of this journey through the world of mainframes are to provide a thorough understanding of their technological evolution, their impact on society and industry, and their enduring legacy in the landscape of computing. This exploration is not just about the machines but about the narrative of human ingenuity, ambition, and the relentless pursuit of technological advancement.

The Evolution of Mainframes: An Overview

The evolution of mainframes is a fascinating chronicle of technological innovation and adaptation. In the early days of computing, mainframes were gigantic machines that filled entire rooms. Despite their size, these early computers were less powerful than even the most basic of today's handheld devices. However, their development over the years has been nothing short of extraordinary, marked by several significant technological milestones.

One of the first major transitions in mainframe technology was the shift from vacuum tubes to transistors. Vacuum tubes, though groundbreaking at their inception, were large, consumed a lot of power, and were prone to frequent overheating. The introduction of transistors revolutionized mainframe design. Transistors were smaller, more reliable, and much more energy-efficient, allowing for the construction of more compact and powerful computers.

The evolution continued with the development of integrated circuits, which took the miniaturization and power efficiency to the next level. Integrated circuits led to the creation of smaller, more powerful, and more reliable systems, which opened up new possibilities in terms of where and how mainframes could be used.

The arrival of microprocessors marked the next major leap. This advancement represented a shift from large-scale integrated circuits to complete processing units on a single chip. Microprocessors enabled even greater processing power and efficiency, further shrinking the size of computers and paving the way for the modern mainframe.

Throughout their evolution, mainframes have been at the forefront of innovations not just in hardware, but also in software. The development of programming languages, from assembly language to high-level languages like COBOL and FORTRAN, was heavily influenced by the needs and capabilities of mainframes. These languages made it possible to write more complex and versatile programs, expanding the range of tasks mainframes could perform.

Networking was another significant development. Early mainframes operated in isolation, but the advent of networking transformed them into connected, collaborative systems. This was critical for the development of distributed computing and the growth of the internet.

In recent times, as cybersecurity emerged as a paramount concern, mainframes have been crucial in developing and implementing robust security protocols. Their ability to handle large-scale, secure transactions made them indispensable in areas like finance and government operations.

Today, in the era of cloud computing and big data analytics, mainframes continue to play a vital role. They have adapted to new paradigms, offering the reliability, security, and processing power necessary for handling vast amounts of data and critical real-time transactions. Far from being relics, modern mainframes are sophisticated systems that form the backbone of many contemporary computing environments.

In summary, the evolution of mainframes is a story of constant reinvention and adaptation. As we delve into this history, we see a technology that has not only survived but thrived by continually evolving to meet the changing needs of the world around it. Mainframes have been a driving force in the development of computing, and they continue to be integral to the infrastructure of our digital world.

Chapter 1: The Birth of Mainframes

The First Giants: Early Computers and Their Limitations

The story of mainframes begins with the first giants of the computing world - the early computers. These initial machines, such as the ENIAC (Electronic Numerical Integrator and Computer) and the Harvard Mark I, were monumental in both their physical size and their impact on technology. ENIAC, for instance, weighed around 30 tons, took up about 1,800 square feet of space, and required a staggering amount of electrical power. These computers used thousands of vacuum tubes for processing and were programmed using a combination of plugboards and switches, making programming a laborious and complex task.

Despite their impressive capabilities for the time, these early computers had significant limitations. They were exceedingly expensive to build and maintain, consumed vast amounts of electricity, and were prone to frequent breakdowns due to the unreliability of vacuum tubes. Their programming and operational processes were not only time-consuming but also required specialized knowledge, limiting their usability to a select few. Moreover, these machines were purpose-built for specific tasks, such as calculations for military use or scientific research, which greatly limited their versatility.

Technological Breakthroughs: Vacuum Tubes to Transistors

The transition from vacuum tubes to transistors marked a revolutionary shift in the computing world. Vacuum tubes, while effective, were large, power-hungry, and prone to failure. The invention of the transistor in 1947 by Bell Laboratories was a game-changer. Transistors were much smaller, more reliable, and consumed far less power than vacuum tubes. This development led to the creation of smaller, more efficient, and more reliable computers.

The first transistorized computer was the TRADIC at Bell Laboratories in 1954, followed by the TX-0 at MIT and the IBM 7090, one of the first commercially produced transistorized computers. These machines represented a significant step forward in computing. They were faster, more energy-efficient, and more stable than their predecessors. This advancement in technology made it possible to start thinking about computers not just as giant calculators for complex scientific tasks but as tools for broader applications in business and government.

The Mainframe in Society: Early Adopters and Impact

The introduction of mainframe computers had a profound impact on society, beginning with their early adopters. In the business world, mainframes allowed for the automation of tasks that were previously manual and time-consuming, such as payroll processing, inventory management, and record keeping. In government, they played a crucial role in census data processing and in the management of large-scale projects such as the Apollo moon missions.

Banks were among the earliest adopters of mainframe technology, using these computers for processing transactions and managing customer accounts more efficiently. This adoption marked the beginning of the digital transformation in the banking industry, which would eventually lead to modern-day online banking.

The use of mainframes also had significant societal implications. They brought about changes in workforce dynamics, creating new roles such as computer operators, programmers, and systems analysts. The capabilities of mainframes also raised questions about data privacy and security, leading to the development of early data protection policies and practices.

In essence, the birth of mainframes was not just the advent of a new technology but the beginning of a new era in computing. This era was characterized by rapid technological advancements and a significant transformation in the way organizations operated and how society at large interacted with technology. As we continue to explore the evolution of mainframes, we uncover the layers of innovation and influence that have made them a cornerstone in the world of computing.

The First Giants: Early Computers and Their Limitations

The advent of mainframe computing is inextricably linked to the colossal and pioneering early computers, which laid the foundation for this technological revolution. These initial forays into the world of computing were marked by machines of unprecedented scale and complexity, such as the ENIAC (Electronic Numerical Integrator and Computer) and the Harvard Mark I.

ENIAC, often cited as the first general-purpose electronic computer, was a behemoth. Weighing around 30 tons and covering about 1,800 square feet, it was a far cry from the compact devices we know today. It utilized approximately 18,000 vacuum tubes for processing, consuming a massive amount of electrical power – enough to light a small town. Programming the ENIAC was a formidable task, involving a complex arrangement of plugboards and switches. This intricate setup meant that reprogramming the machine for different tasks could take days, limiting its flexibility.

Similarly, the Harvard Mark I, another early computer, was an electromechanical monster. It was 51 feet long and eight feet high, consisting of about 760,000 components. The machine operated using a sequence of mechanical and electrical components, making it slower than purely electronic computers like the ENIAC, but it was a significant step towards automatic computing.

The limitations of these early computers, however, were as notable as their innovations. The construction and maintenance costs were astronomical, making them accessible only to well-funded government institutions or large corporations. Their enormous appetite for electricity, along with the heat generated by thousands of vacuum tubes, presented substantial operational challenges.

Moreover, the vacuum tubes, which were the core of these computers' processing power, were prone to frequent failures. A single burnt-out tube could halt the entire machine, leading to considerable downtime and maintenance challenges. This lack of reliability was a significant impediment to the practical use of these computers for critical tasks.

Another limitation was the programming and operational processes of these early machines. Programming was not done through a coded language but rather through physical manipulation of the machine's components. This method was not only time-consuming and laborious but also required highly specialized knowledge, making it inaccessible to the general populace.

Additionally, the early computers were designed for specific, often singular purposes. For instance, ENIAC was initially built to calculate artillery firing tables for the United States Army's Ballistic Research Laboratory. The Harvard Mark I was used for a range of military and scientific applications, including computations for the Manhattan Project. This specificity of purpose meant that these computers lacked versatility, a key feature that would later become a defining characteristic of mainframes.

In summary, while the first giants of the computing world were monumental achievements, they were also hampered by significant limitations in terms of cost, efficiency, reliability, flexibility, and accessibility. These limitations set the stage for the evolution of computing technology, driving the innovations that would lead to the development of the more versatile, reliable, and powerful mainframe computers.

Technological Breakthroughs: Vacuum Tubes to Transistors

The transition from vacuum tubes to transistors stands as one of the most significant milestones in the history of computing technology. This evolution was not just a step but a giant leap forward, bringing about a radical transformation in the design, functionality, and application of computers.

The Limitations of Vacuum Tubes

Before transistors, vacuum tubes were the heart of early computers. These tubes, which controlled electronic signals, were the primary method of data processing and storage. However, they came with a host of drawbacks. Vacuum tubes were bulky, making the computers of the time massive and unwieldy. They were notorious for generating a significant amount of heat, often leading to overheating issues. This heat generation required elaborate cooling systems, further complicating the computer design. Additionally, vacuum tubes consumed a substantial amount of power, making early computers expensive to operate. Perhaps the most critical drawback was their unreliability – vacuum tubes burned out frequently, leading to frequent maintenance and downtime.

The Revolutionary Advent of Transistors

The invention of the transistor in 1947 by a team of scientists at Bell Laboratories revolutionized this landscape. A transistor, essentially a semiconductor device capable of amplifying or switching electronic signals, was far superior to the vacuum tube in every critical aspect. It was significantly smaller, leading to a drastic reduction in the size of computers. Transistors consumed much less power and were more reliable, with a longer operational lifespan than vacuum tubes.

This innovation marked the beginning of the end for vacuum-tube-based computers and ushered in a new era of more compact, efficient, and reliable machines. With transistors, computers no longer needed the massive infrastructure that was previously a necessity. This development opened the door to a broader range of applications and environments for computers.

The Dawn of Transistorized Computers

The first computer to use this groundbreaking technology was the TRADIC (Transistorized Airborne Digital Computer) at Bell Laboratories in 1954, which utilized more than 800 transistors. Following TRADIC, the TX-0 (Transistorized Experimental computer zero) was developed at MIT. It was one of the earliest fully transistorized computers and played a significant role in advancing computer programming and operating systems.

A pivotal moment in the mainstream adoption of transistorized computers was the introduction of the IBM 7090, one of the first commercially produced transistorized computers. The IBM 7090 was a clear departure from its vacuum-tube predecessors in terms of size, speed, and efficiency. It was capable of performing millions of calculations per second, a feat that was unimaginable with vacuum tube computers.

The Broader Impact of Transistorized Computing

The adoption of transistors in computing brought about more than just technical improvements. It marked the start of a new era where computers began to move beyond government and scientific applications to more widespread use in business and industry. The reduced size and increased reliability of computers made them more accessible and practical for a variety of new applications. Businesses began to explore the potential of computers for data processing, inventory management, and even complex decision-making tasks.

In summary, the shift from vacuum tubes to transistors was a fundamental turning point in the history of computing. It paved the way for the development of modern computers, both in terms of technology and the expansion of their role in society. This breakthrough laid the groundwork for the next generation of computing innovations and set the stage for the arrival of mainframe computers, which would further transform the technological landscape.

The Mainframe in Society: Early Adopters and Impact

The advent of mainframe computers marked a watershed moment in the annals of technology, significantly influencing both the business world and government operations. Their impact, however, extended beyond mere technological advancements, reshaping societal structures and introducing new paradigms in data management and privacy.

Transforming the Business Landscape

In the business world, mainframes were a catalyst for a revolution. Large corporations quickly recognized the potential of these powerful machines. For tasks that were once labor-intensive and error-prone, such as payroll processing, inventory management, and financial record keeping, mainframes offered an automated, efficient, and reliable alternative. This automation led to increased productivity, accuracy in data processing, and allowed for the handling of more complex tasks that were previously unmanageable.

Industries such as manufacturing and retail also reaped the benefits of mainframe technology. They could now manage vast inventories and complex supply chains more effectively, enabling them to scale operations and optimize efficiency. The automation of these processes fundamentally changed business operations, leading to new business models and strategies.

Mainframes in Banking and Finance

Banks were among the earliest and most impactful adopters of mainframe technology. They utilized these computers for processing a large number of transactions and managing customer accounts with greater efficiency and accuracy. This adoption marked the dawn of a new era in the banking industry, laying the groundwork for what would eventually evolve into modern-day electronic and online banking. Mainframes enabled banks to offer new services such as ATMs and online transaction processing, transforming the way customers interacted with financial institutions.

Government and Mainframes

In government, mainframes played a pivotal role in various administrative and strategic operations. One of the most notable applications was in census data processing, where the ability to handle and analyze large datasets revolutionized demographic studies and policymaking. Mainframes were also instrumental in scientific research and space exploration, with their most notable contribution being in the management of the Apollo moon missions. These missions required processing vast amounts of data and complex computations that only mainframes could handle at the time.

Societal Implications and Workforce Changes

The introduction of mainframes initiated significant changes in workforce dynamics. New professional roles emerged, such as computer operators, programmers, systems analysts, and database administrators. The demand for skilled professionals in these areas spurred the development of specialized educational and training programs, giving rise to a new sector in the workforce.

Data Privacy and Security Concerns

As mainframes became repositories of vast amounts of personal and sensitive data, they raised concerns about data privacy and security. Businesses and governments were collecting and storing unprecedented quantities of data, leading to the development of early data protection policies and practices. This period marked the beginning of an ongoing conversation about the ethical and legal aspects of data storage and usage, a conversation that remains highly relevant today.

Conclusion

The impact of mainframes in the early stages of their introduction was profound and multifaceted. They revolutionized business processes, government operations, and banking, leading to new efficiencies and capabilities. At the same time, they brought to the fore issues related to data privacy, security, and workforce transformation. The early adoption of mainframes set the stage for the digital era, heralding a new age of technology that would continue to evolve and shape the modern world.

Chapter 2: The Golden Age of Mainframes

The Rise of Business Computing

The 'Golden Age of Mainframes' is characterized by their proliferation into the business world. This era saw a dramatic shift in how businesses operated, with mainframes at the heart of this transformation. During the 1960s and 1970s, businesses across various sectors began to realize the potential of mainframes in streamlining operations and enhancing productivity. This period marked the beginning of widespread business computing.

Corporations harnessed mainframes for a variety of tasks, from managing large datasets and handling complex accounting tasks to processing transactions and managing supply chains. Industries like banking, insurance, retail, and manufacturing were among the first to integrate mainframes into their core operations. This integration allowed for more efficient data processing, better customer service, and strategic decision-making based on data analysis.

This era also saw the development of specialized software and applications for business purposes, including the first database management systems and enterprise resource planning (ERP) systems. These innovations made it possible to handle ever-increasing volumes of data and complex, interrelated business processes, further entrenching mainframes as an indispensable part of the business infrastructure.

Mainframe Architecture: Design and Development

The golden age was also marked by significant advancements in mainframe architecture. Manufacturers focused on making mainframes more powerful, reliable, and efficient. This period saw the development of key architectural concepts like virtualization, which allowed for the more efficient use of computing resources and paved the way for future cloud computing technologies.

Mainframes began to support multiprogramming, where several programs could run concurrently, vastly improving the efficiency and throughput of computing tasks. This was coupled with advancements in storage technology, such as the development of disk storage, which offered faster and more flexible data access compared to previous tape-based storage.

Manufacturers also focused on enhancing the usability and accessibility of mainframes. User-friendly interfaces were developed, and the use of high-level programming languages became more prevalent. These languages made it easier to write and maintain complex programs, broadening the pool of people who could effectively program mainframes.

Mainframes and the Public: Accessibility and Influence

The influence of mainframes extended beyond the business and governmental sectors, starting to touch the public in more direct ways. Public utilities, healthcare, and education began to leverage mainframes for better service delivery. For instance, mainframes played a crucial role in the administration of new and expansive healthcare systems and educational programs.

Additionally, the emergence of automated teller machines (ATMs) in the late 1960s, powered by mainframe computers, revolutionized the banking experience for the general public. This was one of the first widespread public interactions with the capabilities of mainframe computing, bringing a previously unseen level of convenience and accessibility to banking services.

Mainframes also influenced public awareness and understanding of computers. Through their application in various sectors, they started demystifying the concept of computing for the general public. Television shows, news articles, and even advertisements began to feature mainframes, slowly integrating them into the public consciousness as vital cogs in the modern world's infrastructure.

Conclusion

The Golden Age of Mainframes was a period of significant growth and innovation. It established the mainframe as a cornerstone of business and government operations and began the process of integrating computing technology into the fabric of everyday life. This era laid the groundwork for many of the technological conveniences we enjoy today and set the stage for the further evolution of computing technology.

The Rise of Business Computing

The Golden Age of Mainframes, primarily the 1960s and 1970s, was a period when the business world underwent a substantial transformation, with mainframes emerging as the driving force. This era is notable for the widespread adoption of mainframes in various industries, revolutionizing how businesses operated and managed information.

Mainframes: The Backbone of Business Operations

During this time, mainframes became integral to businesses for managing large datasets and executing complex computational tasks. Their ability to handle vast amounts of data with speed and accuracy was unprecedented. Industries like banking, insurance, retail, and manufacturing were pioneers in adopting this technology, integrating mainframes into their core operations.

In banking, mainframes facilitated faster and more efficient transaction processing, which was vital for the industry's expansion and the introduction of new services. Insurance companies used mainframes to manage policies, claims, and actuarial calculations. In retail, mainframes were instrumental in inventory management and sales tracking, helping large retailers manage extensive networks of stores and supply chains. Manufacturing companies leveraged mainframes for everything from supply chain management to automating various aspects of the production process.

Facilitating Efficient Data Processing and Customer Service

One of the key advantages of mainframes was their capacity to process large volumes of data rapidly. This capability allowed businesses to gain insights from their data like never before. Companies could track trends, forecast demands, and make informed strategic decisions. This enhanced decision-making process contributed significantly to increased operational efficiency and competitive advantage.

Moreover, mainframes played a critical role in improving customer service. They enabled faster and more accurate processing of customer data, leading to more personalized and efficient services. This transformation was particularly evident in sectors like banking and retail, where customer service is paramount.

Development of Specialized Software and Applications

This era also witnessed the birth and growth of specialized business software. The development of the first database management systems marked a significant milestone. These systems allowed for organized and efficient handling of large databases, a task that was previously cumbersome and prone to errors.

Similarly, the introduction of Enterprise Resource Planning (ERP) systems was a game-changer. ERP systems integrated various business processes, from accounting to inventory management, into a unified, mainframe-based system. This integration allowed for unprecedented coordination and efficiency in business operations.

Impact on Business Infrastructure

The adoption of mainframes necessitated changes in business infrastructure. Companies had to invest in hardware and software, and more importantly, in training employees to operate and manage these new systems. This investment was significant, but the returns in terms of efficiency, accuracy, and capability were enormous.

In conclusion, the rise of business computing during the Golden Age of Mainframes marked a turning point in the history of technology and business. Mainframes transformed how businesses operated, managed data, and served customers. They laid the foundation for the modern digital business landscape and set the stage for the subsequent developments in computing technology. This era was not just about technological advancement; it was about a paradigm shift in the way businesses thought about and utilized data.

Mainframe Architecture: Design and Development

During the Golden Age of Mainframes, there was a concentrated effort to enhance mainframe architecture, focusing on increasing power, reliability, and efficiency. This period was marked by groundbreaking advancements that not only revolutionized mainframe design but also laid the foundation for many modern computing concepts.

Virtualization: A Pathway to Efficient Computing

One of the key architectural innovations of this era was the development of virtualization. Virtualization allowed a single mainframe to simulate multiple computing environments, thereby maximizing the use of its computing resources. This meant that different applications and processes could run in separate virtual environments on the same physical machine, leading to more efficient resource utilization and reducing the need for multiple physical machines.

The concept of virtualization was revolutionary. It enabled businesses to scale their computing needs without corresponding increases in physical hardware, significantly reducing costs and space requirements. This technology was a precursor to the cloud computing technologies that dominate the modern digital landscape.

Multiprogramming: Boosting Efficiency and Throughput

Another significant advancement was the support for multiprogramming. Early computers could only execute one program at a time. Multiprogramming changed this, allowing for several programs to run concurrently on the same machine. This capability dramatically improved the efficiency and throughput of computing tasks.

Multiprogramming meant that mainframes could handle multiple tasks simultaneously, reducing idle time and increasing overall productivity. This was particularly beneficial in business and research environments, where the ability to process multiple tasks quickly and accurately was paramount.

Advancements in Storage Technology

This era also saw significant improvements in mainframe storage technology. The move from tape-based to disk-based storage was a pivotal development. Disk storage offered faster and more flexible access to data compared to tape storage, which was sequential and slower.

Disk storage enabled random access to data, allowing for quicker retrieval and processing. This was crucial for businesses that needed timely access to large amounts of data, like financial institutions and large retailers. The increased storage capacity and speed significantly enhanced the overall functionality of mainframes.

Enhancing Usability and Accessibility

As mainframes became more complex, there was a growing need to make them more user-friendly. This need led to the development of more sophisticated user interfaces. These interfaces were designed to be more intuitive, making it easier for operators to manage and control mainframe operations.

Simultaneously, there was a shift towards the use of high-level programming languages. Unlike machine code or assembly language, high-level languages were closer to natural language and therefore more accessible to a broader range of programmers. This shift not only made it easier to write and maintain complex programs but also expanded the pool of people who could effectively program mainframes. Languages like COBOL and FORTRAN became synonymous with mainframe programming, simplifying the development of business and scientific applications.

Conclusion

The architectural advancements during the Golden Age of Mainframes were critical in shaping the future of computing. These developments not only enhanced the capabilities and efficiency of mainframes but also introduced concepts that are fundamental to today's computing landscape. The innovations in virtualization, multiprogramming, storage, and user interfaces during this period laid the groundwork for the evolution of mainframes into the powerful, versatile machines that are still in use today.

Mainframes and the Public: Accessibility and Influence

During the Golden Age of Mainframes, the influence of these powerful computers began to permeate more visibly into everyday life, marking a shift from their traditional confines of business and government operations. Mainframes started to play an integral role in sectors directly impacting the public, such as utilities, healthcare, and education, thereby reshaping service delivery and public interaction with technology.

Enhancing Public Utilities and Services

Mainframes were instrumental in revolutionizing public utility services. Utility companies began using mainframes to manage complex data related to water supply, electricity, and gas services. This data management enabled more efficient resource distribution, billing, and customer service. The reliability and processing power of mainframes ensured that these essential services could be delivered consistently and without interruption, a critical aspect for public utilities.

In healthcare, mainframes facilitated the management of expansive healthcare systems. They were used for storing and processing patient records, managing hospital and clinic schedules, and even in research for disease tracking and epidemiology. Mainframes allowed healthcare providers to access and analyze patient data quickly, leading to more informed and timely medical decisions and treatments.

The field of education also saw a transformation through mainframe computing. Universities and educational institutions began using mainframes for administrative purposes, such as student registrations, grades management, and course scheduling. Additionally, mainframes enabled the development and administration of new educational programs and research projects, opening new avenues for learning and discovery.

Revolutionizing Banking with ATMs

One of the most public-facing impacts of mainframes was in the banking sector with the introduction of Automated Teller Machines (ATMs) in the late 1960s. These ATMs, powered by mainframes, changed the face of banking for the average consumer. For the first time, customers could conduct financial transactions like withdrawals and deposits outside of traditional banking hours and without human interaction.

This development not only provided unprecedented convenience and accessibility but also introduced the public to the capabilities of computerized services. The widespread adoption of ATMs was a significant step in familiarizing the general populace with digital technology and its potential to simplify and improve everyday tasks.

Influencing Public Perception and Awareness

The expanding role of mainframes in various public sectors played a crucial part in shaping the public's perception and understanding of computers. Mainframes began to be featured more prominently in the media – in television shows, news articles, and advertisements. These depictions demystified the concept of computing, gradually educating and acclimating the public to the presence and benefits of these technologies in their daily lives.

Mainframes, through their various applications, started to be recognized not just as tools for businesses and government but as essential components of modern infrastructure, crucial for the functioning of a technologically advanced society.

Conclusion

In summary, the influence of mainframes during their golden age extended significantly into the public sphere, bringing about transformative changes in service delivery and public interaction with technology. This period marked a turning point in how the general public perceived and interacted with computing technology, setting the stage for the ubiquitous presence of digital technology in contemporary life. Mainframes, through their versatile and powerful applications, played a pivotal role in ushering in this new era of public engagement with technology.

Chapter 3: The Changing Landscape

The Advent of Personal Computers: A Shift in the Market

The landscape of computing underwent a significant transformation with the advent of personal computers (PCs) in the late 1970s and early 1980s. This new category of computers, epitomized by the Apple II, the IBM PC, and later by various MS-DOS and Windows-based machines, brought computing into the homes and offices of everyday users. The PC revolution marked a paradigm shift in the market, drastically changing the perception and accessibility of computing technology.

Personal computers, being much more affordable and user-friendly than mainframes, quickly gained popularity. They democratized access to computing, allowing small businesses and individual consumers to benefit from digital technology. This shift posed a new challenge for mainframes, as PCs began to take over tasks that were once the sole domain of larger computers.

Mainframes vs. Minicomputers: A New Competition

Parallel to the rise of PCs was the emergence of minicomputers, a class of smaller, less expensive, and more accessible computers that bridged the gap between mainframes and PCs. Minicomputers like the PDP-11 and the VAX series from Digital Equipment Corporation (DEC) became popular in scientific research, engineering, and business settings. They offered a compelling balance of performance, size, and cost, making them suitable for tasks that did not require the full power or expense of a mainframe.

This period saw an intense competition between mainframes and minicomputers. Minicomputers began to encroach on the market share of mainframes by offering a more affordable and accessible option for medium-scale computing tasks. Mainframe manufacturers faced the challenge of justifying the higher costs and complexity of their machines in light of these emerging alternatives.

Adapting to Change: Mainframe Evolution in the PC Era

In response to these market changes, mainframe technology underwent significant evolution. Mainframe manufacturers focused on leveraging the strengths of their machines—reliability, security, and the ability to handle large volumes of transactions and data. They invested in developing more powerful and efficient systems, incorporating advancements in technology to maintain their relevance in an increasingly competitive market.

One key area of development was in enhancing the connectivity and compatibility of mainframes with PCs and minicomputers. The idea was to enable mainframes to serve as central hubs in networked environments, where they could effectively manage and process data from a multitude of sources, including PCs and minicomputers.

Another focus was on improving the user experience and ease of use of mainframes. This period saw the development of more sophisticated operating systems and user interfaces, making mainframes more accessible to a broader range of users. Mainframe manufacturers also started offering more customized solutions, tailoring their systems to meet the specific needs of different industries and applications.

Mainframes also began to integrate with emerging technologies such as the internet and early forms of cloud computing, further solidifying their position as essential components in the computing ecosystem. Despite the rise of PCs and minicomputers, mainframes remained vital in sectors that required high levels of data processing power and reliability, such as banking, telecommunications, and large-scale enterprise operations.

Conclusion

The advent of personal computers and minicomputers marked a pivotal moment in the history of computing, bringing new challenges and opportunities to the world of mainframes. This era was characterized by adaptation and evolution, as mainframe technology continued to advance and find its place in the changing landscape of computing. The resilience and adaptability of mainframes during this period underscored their enduring significance in the computing world.

The Advent of Personal Computers: A Shift in the Market

The emergence of personal computers (PCs) in the late 1970s and early 1980s signaled a seismic shift in the computing landscape, fundamentally altering the dynamics of the market and how society interacted with technology. This era marked the transition from an age where computers were predominantly large, expensive mainframe systems accessible to only businesses and institutions, to a new era where computing power became available to the masses.

The Birth of the PC Era

The introduction of the Apple II in 1977, followed by the IBM PC in 1981, and the subsequent proliferation of MS-DOS and Windows-based machines, represented more than just the arrival of new technology. These machines symbolized the democratization of computing. Unlike the room-sized mainframes, these PCs were compact enough to fit on a desk and simple enough for use by individuals without specialized training.

PCs like the Apple II and IBM PC offered a previously unimaginable level of accessibility to computing power. They came equipped with user-friendly interfaces, making them appealing to a broad audience, including those without a technical background. This accessibility was further enhanced by the development of graphical user interfaces, which made PCs even more intuitive to use.

A Market Transformed

The affordability of PCs was a critical factor in their widespread adoption. While mainframes and minicomputers cost tens or hundreds of thousands of dollars, PCs were available at a fraction of this price, putting them within reach of small businesses and individual consumers. This price difference opened up a whole new market segment, allowing those who could never before afford computing power to integrate it into their daily lives and business operations.

The impact of PCs on the market was profound. Small businesses began to leverage these new tools for a variety of purposes, from accounting to inventory management. Individuals used PCs for everything from word processing and education to gaming and personal finance. This widespread adoption began to erode the market for mainframes, as tasks that previously required large-scale computing power could now be handled by these smaller, more affordable machines.

Challenges for Mainframes

The rise of PCs posed a significant challenge to the mainframe industry. Tasks like data processing, once the exclusive domain of mainframes, were now being taken over by PCs and networks of PCs. Mainframe manufacturers faced the daunting task of redefining the role of their machines in an era where computing was rapidly becoming more personal and decentralized.

In response, mainframe manufacturers began to pivot, focusing on the strengths of their machines. They emphasized the ability of mainframes to handle large-scale transactions and process vast amounts of data reliably - tasks that PCs were not equipped to manage. Mainframes continued to be essential in areas where high-performance computing was crucial, such as in large corporations, banks, and government institutions.

Conclusion

The advent of personal computers marked a turning point in the history of computing, heralding a new age of accessibility and widespread adoption. This era did not spell the end for mainframes but rather set the stage for their evolution. As PCs took over the lower end of the market, mainframes began to solidify their role in handling more demanding computational tasks, showcasing the adaptability and resilience of this enduring technology.

Mainframes vs. Minicomputers: A New Competition

As personal computers began reshaping the consumer end of the computing spectrum, another significant development was unfolding in the realm of business and scientific computing: the rise of minicomputers. This new class of computers emerged as a formidable middle ground between the colossal mainframes and the nascent personal computers, sparking a new competitive dynamic in the industry.

Emergence of Minicomputers

Minicomputers, epitomized by systems like the PDP-11 and the VAX series from Digital Equipment Corporation (DEC), brought a new dimension to the computing landscape in the 1970s and 1980s. These machines were smaller, less expensive, and more accessible compared to traditional mainframes. Despite their reduced size and cost, minicomputers were powerful enough to handle significant computational tasks that were previously the domain of larger mainframe computers.

The appeal of minicomputers lay in their ability to offer a balanced combination of performance, size, and cost. They were capable enough to meet the computing needs of medium-sized businesses, research institutions, and engineering projects without the substantial investment required for a mainframe. This made them particularly attractive in environments where the high capacity of a mainframe was not necessary, or where budget constraints made mainframes an impractical choice.

Intensifying Competition

The popularity of minicomputers began to challenge the dominance of mainframes in several sectors. In scientific research and engineering, minicomputers became the preferred choice due to their adequate computing power and more accessible programming environments. Businesses, especially small to medium-sized enterprises, started opting for minicomputers for tasks like data processing, inventory management, and financial accounting.

This shift posed a significant challenge to mainframe manufacturers. The primary selling points of mainframes — their processing power and capacity to handle large-scale computational tasks — were being effectively countered by the more affordable and suitably powerful minicomputers. Mainframe manufacturers found themselves in a position where they had to justify the higher costs and complexity of their systems.

Response of Mainframe Manufacturers

In response to this growing competition, mainframe manufacturers began to innovate and adapt. They focused on enhancing the features that set mainframes apart: superior processing power, reliability, and the ability to handle vast amounts of data and transactions. Mainframes were positioned as the go-to solution for large enterprises and critical applications where the capabilities of minicomputers fell short.

Moreover, mainframe manufacturers started to streamline their operations and reduce costs to remain competitive. They also began integrating new technologies and features into mainframes, such as improved networking capabilities and user interfaces, making them more versatile and easier to use.

Conclusion

The competition between mainframes and minicomputers marked a pivotal phase in the evolution of computing technology. It spurred innovation and diversification in the market, leading to more choices for businesses and institutions. This era highlighted the dynamic nature of the technology sector, where new advancements continuously reshape the competitive landscape. Mainframes, in adapting to these changes, demonstrated their resilience and enduring relevance in the world of computing.

Adapting to Change: Mainframe Evolution in the PC Era

The advent of personal computers and minicomputers presented a formidable challenge to the mainframe industry, prompting a period of significant evolution and adaptation. Mainframe manufacturers were compelled to innovate and reposition their products to maintain relevance in a rapidly evolving market characterized by increasing competition and changing customer needs.

Leveraging Core Strengths

Mainframe manufacturers recognized the need to emphasize and build upon the inherent strengths of their machines. The key attributes of mainframes – their reliability, security, and ability to handle large volumes of transactions and data – were more crucial than ever. This period saw significant investments in improving the processing power and efficiency of mainframes. Manufacturers worked on enhancing the speed and capacity of these machines, ensuring they remained the most powerful computing option available, especially for tasks requiring extensive data processing and high-level security.

Enhancing Connectivity and Compatibility

A pivotal area of development was enhancing the connectivity and compatibility of mainframes with the emerging ecosystem of PCs and minicomputers. The objective was to transform mainframes from isolated computing behemoths to central hubs in increasingly networked and distributed computing environments. By doing so, mainframes could serve as the backbone of complex IT infrastructures, managing and processing data from a variety of sources, including PCs and minicomputers.

This shift involved significant advancements in networking technologies and the development of new protocols and interfaces that facilitated seamless communication between mainframes and other types of computers. It allowed businesses to integrate their mainframe systems with their growing networks of PCs, enabling more flexible and comprehensive IT solutions.

Improving User Experience and Customization

Another focus for mainframe manufacturers was improving the user experience. This era witnessed the development of more sophisticated and user-friendly operating systems and interfaces for mainframes. Efforts were made to make these systems more intuitive and accessible, reducing the steep learning curve traditionally associated with mainframe operation and broadening their appeal to a wider user base.

Customization also became a key strategy. Manufacturers began offering more tailored solutions, designing systems that catered to the specific needs of different industries and applications. This bespoke approach allowed mainframes to better serve unique industry requirements, from banking and finance to healthcare and government operations.

Integration with Emerging Technologies

Mainframes also started to integrate with cutting-edge technologies like the internet and early cloud computing forms. This integration was critical in positioning mainframes as vital components in the burgeoning digital landscape. By embracing these new technologies, mainframes could support a wider range of applications, from web-based services to early cloud storage and processing solutions.

Mainframes in the Modern Computing Landscape

Despite the proliferation of PCs and the growing popularity of minicomputers, mainframes retained their importance in sectors where high levels of data processing power, reliability, and security were paramount. Industries such as banking, telecommunications, and large-scale enterprise operations continued to rely on mainframes as the backbone of their computing infrastructure.

Conclusion

The PC era brought about a significant shift in the computing landscape, challenging the mainframe industry to evolve and adapt. Through a combination of technological advancements, enhanced connectivity, improved user experience, and integration with new technologies, mainframes successfully navigated this period of change. This adaptability not only affirmed the resilience of mainframe technology but also cemented its ongoing relevance in an increasingly diverse and dynamic computing world.

Chapter 4: The Era of Connectivity

Networking and the Internet: A New Role for Mainframes

As the world entered the era of connectivity, mainframes found a new and crucial role in the evolving digital landscape. The emergence of widespread networking and the advent of the internet in the late 20th century opened new frontiers for mainframe computing. Rather than being phased out, mainframes adapted to become central figures in this new era.

Mainframes played a pivotal role in the development and expansion of networking and internet infrastructures. Their ability to process large volumes of data efficiently made them ideal for managing the complex networks that form the backbone of the internet. Mainframes were used to control network traffic, manage large databases, and support critical online applications and services.

This period saw mainframes becoming key players in the transition from isolated computing systems to interconnected networks. They adapted to support new networking protocols and interfaces, ensuring that they could communicate seamlessly with a wide array of networked devices and systems. This capability enabled mainframes to serve as central servers in large-scale networked environments, managing critical aspects of data exchange and communication.

Mainframes in the Digital Age: Powering the Web

The rise of the World Wide Web further expanded the role of mainframes. As businesses and organizations sought to establish their online presence, mainframes became the go-to solution for hosting large, complex websites and supporting web-based applications. Their robust processing capabilities were ideal for handling the high traffic volumes and large-scale data processing required by major websites.

Mainframes also played a significant role in e-commerce, supporting the databases and transaction-processing systems that underpin online shopping platforms. Their reliability and ability to handle massive transaction volumes made them indispensable in this rapidly growing sector.

Moreover, as cloud computing began to emerge, mainframes adapted once again. They became integral to the infrastructure of cloud services, offering a secure and reliable platform for cloud providers to host their services and data. The scalability and processing power of mainframes made them well-suited for the demands of cloud computing.

Security and Reliability: The Unseen Backbone

Throughout the era of connectivity, mainframes remained synonymous with security and reliability – two attributes that became increasingly important in a digitally interconnected world. As cyber threats evolved and data breaches became a significant concern, the inherent security features of mainframes made them a trusted choice for industries handling sensitive data.

Mainframes' ability to facilitate secure transactions and protect large volumes of sensitive data made them essential in sectors like finance, healthcare, and government. Their robust security protocols and advanced encryption capabilities provided a level of protection that was difficult to match.

Additionally, the unmatched reliability of mainframes was critical in applications where uptime was crucial. In scenarios where downtime could result in significant disruptions or losses, such as in financial trading or airline reservation systems, mainframes offered the necessary dependability.

Conclusion

The era of connectivity did not render mainframes obsolete; instead, it redefined their role in the computing world. Mainframes adapted to become fundamental components in networking and the internet infrastructure, powering key elements of the digital age from web services to cloud computing. Their evolution in terms of connectivity, security, and reliability underscored their enduring relevance and importance in an increasingly connected and digital world.

Networking and the Internet: A New Role for Mainframes

As the digital world expanded into the era of connectivity, mainframes experienced a renaissance, reinventing themselves as indispensable players in the burgeoning landscape of networking and the internet. Far from becoming obsolete, mainframes adapted to the changing technological climate, carving out a new, critical role for themselves in this connected era.

Facilitating the Growth of Networking and the Internet

The late 20th century witnessed explosive growth in networking and the birth of the internet, leading to a dramatic increase in data communication and processing needs. Mainframes, with their robust processing capabilities, stepped up to meet these demands. They were uniquely suited to handle the high volumes of data and the complex operations required for managing and maintaining the growing network infrastructures that would form the internet's backbone.

Mainframes became instrumental in controlling network traffic, ensuring efficient and smooth data flow across global networks. They managed complex tasks such as load balancing, routing, and network security. Their ability to process and analyze large datasets quickly made them ideal for overseeing extensive networks and ensuring optimal performance.

Transition to Interconnected Networks

One of the most significant adaptations of mainframes in this era was their integration into interconnected network environments. Previously seen as standalone behemoths, mainframes evolved to support new networking protocols and interfaces, allowing them to communicate effectively with a variety of networked devices and systems.

This evolution was critical in transitioning mainframes from isolated computing units to central servers in complex, distributed networks. They began to serve as the nerve centers of these networks, handling data exchange, storage, and processing. Mainframes' reliability and high-capacity processing power made them invaluable for businesses and organizations relying on the uninterrupted flow of data.

Mainframes as Central Servers in Networked Environments

Mainframes found a renewed purpose as central servers, especially in large-scale networked environments such as corporate intranets and enterprise IT systems. They managed not only the flow of internal data but also the interfaces with external networks, including the internet. Their robust architecture allowed them to handle multiple tasks concurrently, from running enterprise applications to managing user access and data security.

In the world of the internet, mainframes contributed significantly to hosting and managing online services and applications. Many of the critical online systems, from banking portals to e-commerce platforms, relied on the power and reliability of mainframe systems to function effectively.

Conclusion

The advent of networking and the internet ushered in a new era for mainframe computing, highlighting their versatility and capacity for adaptation. Far from being sidelined by newer technologies, mainframes evolved to become central to the infrastructure of the connected world. Their ability to handle vast data volumes, manage complex network tasks, and ensure high levels of security and reliability underpinned the growth and functionality of networking and internet services. In this era of connectivity, mainframes proved not only their resilience but also their enduring relevance and importance in the ever-evolving landscape of digital technology.

Mainframes in the Digital Age: Powering the Web

With the rise of the World Wide Web in the 1990s and early 2000s, the digital age witnessed an unprecedented expansion in the role of mainframes. As the web evolved into an essential part of business and daily life, mainframes adapted to become pivotal in powering the burgeoning online world.

Hosting Websites and Web-Based Applications

As businesses and organizations rushed to establish their presence on the World Wide Web, the demand for robust, reliable hosting solutions soared. Mainframes emerged as the premier choice for hosting large and complex websites. Their robust processing capabilities made them exceptionally suited for handling the high traffic volumes these websites attracted.

Mainframes excelled in managing the demanding data processing needs of major online portals, corporate websites, and information hubs. Their ability to efficiently process and serve massive amounts of data concurrently meant that businesses could rely on them to provide uninterrupted access to their online services, even during peak traffic times.

E-Commerce and Transaction Processing

The digital age also marked the rapid growth of e-commerce, transforming how businesses sold products and services and how consumers shopped. Mainframes played a critical role in this transformation. They supported the sophisticated databases and transaction-processing systems that are the backbone of online shopping platforms.

Their reliability and capacity to handle enormous transaction volumes without faltering made mainframes an indispensable asset in e-commerce. They ensured smooth, secure, and fast transaction processing, which was crucial for maintaining consumer trust and satisfaction in the online shopping experience.

Integration with Cloud Computing

As cloud computing began to take shape as the next frontier in digital services, mainframes demonstrated their adaptability once more. They became integral components of the infrastructure that supports cloud services. Cloud computing demanded a combination of scalability, reliability, and processing power – qualities inherent in mainframe technology.

Mainframes offered a secure and reliable platform for cloud providers, enabling them to host a variety of services and manage large datasets. They could support the dynamic scaling of resources, making them suitable for cloud environments where demand can fluctuate dramatically. This capability ensured that cloud services remained responsive and reliable, regardless of the workload.

Conclusion

In the digital age, characterized by the explosion of the World Wide Web and the advent of cloud computing, mainframes have proved not only their resilience but also their critical importance. They have continued to adapt and evolve, meeting the demands of an increasingly connected and digital world. From hosting complex websites to powering e-commerce and cloud services, mainframes have remained at the forefront of the digital revolution, underpinning the technologies that drive our modern digital experiences.

Security and Reliability: The Unseen Backbone

In the digital age, particularly during the era of connectivity, mainframes solidified their reputation as the bedrock of security and reliability in the computing world. These two attributes became increasingly vital as the digital landscape expanded, bringing with it a surge in cyber threats and the need for secure data handling.

Mainframes as Bastions of Security

As the frequency and sophistication of cyber-attacks grew, the inherent security features of mainframes positioned them as the ideal choice for industries dealing with sensitive and critical data. Mainframes have been designed with robust security measures at their core, providing a level of data protection that few other systems can match.

One of the key strengths of mainframes in terms of security is their advanced encryption capabilities. Mainframes can encrypt data at a scale and speed unattainable by other types of computing systems. This feature is crucial for protecting vast quantities of data, a common requirement in sectors like finance, healthcare, and government operations.

In the finance sector, mainframes safeguard transaction data and personal financial information, offering a secure platform for online banking, trading, and other financial services. In healthcare, they protect sensitive patient records, ensuring compliance with stringent privacy regulations. For government agencies, mainframes secure confidential data and support critical public services.

Ensuring Unmatched Reliability and Uptime

The reliability of mainframes is another key factor in their enduring importance. In a world where downtime can have far-reaching consequences, the dependability of mainframes is invaluable. They are engineered to handle high-volume, mission-critical workloads with minimal interruption, making them indispensable in sectors where operational continuity is paramount.

In the financial world, mainframes support the uninterrupted functioning of trading systems and transaction processing, where even a brief downtime can result in significant financial losses. In airline operations, mainframes manage reservation and scheduling systems, ensuring smooth and reliable service to millions of passengers.

The design of mainframes inherently focuses on minimizing downtime. Features such as redundant hardware components, sophisticated error-checking algorithms, and automated failover processes ensure that mainframes continue to operate smoothly, even under adverse conditions.

Adapting to an Evolving Digital Landscape

As the digital landscape continues to evolve, mainframes adapt alongside it, continuously enhancing their security and reliability features. They have proven to be adept at addressing emerging threats and adapting to changing technological requirements, maintaining their status as the backbone of secure and reliable computing in a highly interconnected world.

Conclusion

In summary, the unmatched security and reliability of mainframes have made them the unseen backbone of many critical industries. They provide a foundation of trust and stability in a digital age marked by increasing threats and the need for secure, uninterrupted operations. As the digital ecosystem grows more complex, the role of mainframes in ensuring secure and reliable computing remains more relevant than ever.

Chapter 5: The Modern Mainframe

Innovations and Current Technologies in Mainframe Computing

In the modern era, mainframe computing has continued to evolve, integrating cutting-edge technologies to stay relevant in a rapidly changing digital landscape. Today's mainframes are far more advanced than their predecessors, boasting incredible processing power, expanded memory capacity, and sophisticated software environments.

One significant innovation in modern mainframes is the integration of artificial intelligence and machine learning capabilities. This advancement allows mainframes to process and analyze massive datasets more efficiently, providing invaluable insights and decision-making support in real-time. Additionally, modern mainframes have embraced the Internet of Things (IoT), processing data from countless devices and sensors in various applications, from industrial automation to smart city infrastructures.

Energy efficiency and eco-friendliness have also become crucial aspects of mainframe development. Newer models are designed to minimize energy consumption and reduce the carbon footprint, aligning with global sustainability goals. Moreover, contemporary mainframes have enhanced connectivity options, supporting a broader range of network protocols and data formats, making them more versatile in heterogeneous IT environments.

Mainframes in the Cloud Era: New Challenges and Opportunities

The advent of cloud computing presented new challenges and opportunities for mainframe computing. Mainframes have adapted to function seamlessly within cloud environments, offering a unique combination of scalability, security, and reliability to cloud service providers and users.

Modern mainframes have become integral to hybrid cloud strategies, where they work in tandem with cloud platforms to provide a comprehensive solution that leverages the strengths of both environments. In this setup, mainframes handle high-volume transactions and sensitive data processing, while the cloud offers flexibility and scalability for less intensive tasks.

This era has also seen the development of mainframe-as-a-service (MaaS) offerings, where mainframe resources are available over the cloud, providing clients with the power of mainframe computing without the need for physical hardware on-site. This model has opened up mainframe computing to a wider range of businesses, particularly those that require mainframe capabilities but lack the infrastructure to support them.

The Future of Mainframes: Predictions and Possibilities

Looking ahead, the future of mainframes appears robust, with ongoing advancements ensuring their continued relevance. One area of potential growth is the increased integration of mainframes with blockchain technology. Mainframes could become key players in managing large-scale blockchain applications, given their ability to process large volumes of transactions securely and efficiently.

Another emerging trend is the use of mainframes in advanced analytics and big data applications. As data volumes continue to grow exponentially, the processing power and reliability of mainframes make them ideal for analyzing this data to glean actionable insights.

In the realm of cybersecurity, mainframes are likely to play an increasingly crucial role. Their ability to securely handle vast amounts of sensitive data makes them an attractive option for organizations looking to bolster their cybersecurity defenses.

Finally, as artificial intelligence and machine learning continue to advance, the role of mainframes in these fields is expected to expand. Mainframes could become central to AI-driven processes, providing the computational muscle needed to train complex models and manage AI workloads.

Conclusion

The modern mainframe has adapted impressively to the challenges and opportunities presented by the digital age. Through continuous innovation and integration with new technologies, mainframes have not only maintained their relevance but have also expanded their role in the computing world. As we look to the future, mainframes are poised to continue evolving, playing a critical role in the development and implementation of cutting-edge technologies.

Innovations and Current Technologies in Mainframe Computing

The landscape of mainframe computing in the modern era is a testament to continuous innovation and adaptation. Today's mainframes are a quantum leap from their early ancestors, boasting formidable processing power and a suite of advanced features that keep them at the forefront of enterprise computing needs.

Integration of AI and Machine Learning

A key innovation in contemporary mainframes is the integration of artificial intelligence (AI) and machine learning (ML). This advancement equips mainframes to handle and analyze enormous datasets with greater efficiency and accuracy. AI and ML enable mainframes to perform complex data analytics, providing real-time insights and decision-making support that are critical in today's fast-paced business environment.

These capabilities are particularly valuable in fields such as finance, where real-time fraud detection can save millions, and in healthcare, where quick analysis of patient data can lead to life-saving diagnoses and treatments. Mainframes equipped with AI and ML algorithms can process vast amounts of data, learning and adapting over time to provide increasingly accurate insights.

Embracing the Internet of Things (IoT)

The modern mainframe has also embraced the Internet of Things (IoT), playing a significant role in processing and analyzing data from a myriad of connected devices and sensors. This functionality is crucial in a wide range of applications, from managing complex industrial automation processes to optimizing smart city infrastructures.

In industrial settings, mainframes can process data from thousands of sensors, providing operational insights and predictive maintenance alerts. In smart cities, they can manage data from traffic sensors, public transport networks, and utility systems, contributing to more efficient urban management.

Energy Efficiency and Sustainability

As global emphasis on sustainability grows, modern mainframes have evolved to become more energy-efficient and eco-friendly. New models are designed to minimize energy use and reduce their carbon footprint, aligning with environmental sustainability goals.

This focus on energy efficiency doesn't just contribute to a greener planet; it also reduces operational costs for businesses. Modern mainframes achieve greater processing power with a lower energy requirement, reducing the total cost of ownership and making them an economically sound choice for large-scale computing needs.

Enhanced Connectivity and Versatility

Contemporary mainframes offer enhanced connectivity options, supporting a diverse range of network protocols and data formats. This makes them highly versatile and capable of functioning in heterogeneous IT environments. They can seamlessly integrate with various systems and platforms, whether it's connecting with cloud services or interfacing with legacy systems.

This adaptability ensures that modern mainframes can continue to serve as the backbone of complex enterprise IT infrastructures, regardless of the varied technologies and platforms used within an organization.

Conclusion

The evolution of mainframe technology in the modern era reflects a commitment to innovation and relevance. With advancements in AI, IoT integration, energy efficiency, and enhanced connectivity, mainframes continue to be indispensable in various sectors, driving efficiency, and providing the computational power necessary to meet today's complex data processing challenges. Their continuous evolution makes them not just survivors of a bygone era but active, vital participants in the ongoing digital revolution.

Mainframes in the Cloud Era: New Challenges and Opportunities

The emergence of cloud computing has significantly reshaped the computing landscape, introducing both challenges and opportunities for mainframe computing. Far from being rendered obsolete, mainframes have adapted to become a vital component of the cloud era, blending their traditional strengths with the new capabilities offered by cloud technology.

Seamless Integration into Cloud Environments

One of the most significant adaptations of mainframes in the cloud era is their ability to function seamlessly within cloud environments. Modern mainframes offer a unique combination of scalability, security, and reliability, which are highly valued in cloud computing. They provide robust back-end support for cloud services, handling complex, high-volume transactions and sensitive data processing that cloud platforms might find challenging.

This integration has allowed mainframes to remain relevant and valuable, even as more businesses and organizations transition to cloud-based solutions. By offering a level of security and processing power that complements the cloud, mainframes continue to be an indispensable asset in the overall IT strategy of many organizations.

Hybrid Cloud Strategies

Modern mainframes have become integral to hybrid cloud strategies, where they are used in conjunction with cloud platforms to create a comprehensive computing solution. In a hybrid cloud environment, the mainframe and cloud systems coexist and collaborate, each playing to its strengths.

The mainframe handles tasks that require its high-level processing capabilities and stringent security measures, such as handling large-scale financial transactions or managing sensitive healthcare data. At the same time, the cloud provides resources for less intensive tasks and offers the flexibility and scalability needed for varying workloads. This hybrid approach allows organizations to enjoy the best of both worlds – the reliability and security of mainframes combined with the agility and resource elasticity of the cloud.

Mainframe-as-a-Service (MaaS)

Another significant development in the cloud era is the advent of Mainframe-as-a-Service (MaaS). This innovative approach allows organizations to utilize mainframe resources over the cloud, eliminating the need to invest in and maintain physical mainframe hardware on-site. MaaS offers businesses the power and capabilities of mainframe computing via a cloud service model, making it more accessible and cost-effective.

This service model is particularly appealing to small and medium-sized businesses that require the robust capabilities of a mainframe but do not have the resources to invest in and manage their own mainframe infrastructure. It also provides an opportunity for companies in sectors like fintech, e-commerce, and healthcare to leverage the power of mainframe computing without the traditional barriers to entry.

Conclusion

The cloud era has brought new life to mainframe computing, allowing it to adapt and thrive amidst the evolving demands of modern technology. By integrating with cloud environments and contributing to hybrid cloud strategies, mainframes have proven their ongoing relevance and value. The development of MaaS has further expanded the reach and accessibility of mainframes, ensuring that they continue to play a crucial role in the computing strategies of a diverse range of industries. Mainframes in the cloud era are not just surviving; they are innovating and expanding, continuing to be a cornerstone of enterprise computing.

The Future of Mainframes: Predictions and Possibilities

The trajectory of mainframe computing is pointing towards continued relevance and innovation, adapting to emerging technologies and evolving business needs. The future of mainframes is not just about maintaining their legacy capabilities but also about expanding into new, cutting-edge domains.

Integration with Blockchain Technology

One promising area of growth for mainframes is their integration with blockchain technology. Given their robust processing capabilities and heightened security features, mainframes are well-suited to become pivotal in managing blockchain applications. Blockchain technology requires the processing of large volumes of transactions while ensuring security and integrity – attributes that are intrinsic to mainframe computing.

Mainframes could play a critical role in sectors like finance, supply chain management, and identity verification, where blockchain applications are rapidly gaining ground. Their ability to handle complex cryptographic processes and manage large-scale distributed ledgers makes them ideal for supporting blockchain infrastructures.

Advancements in Big Data and Analytics

As the volume of data generated worldwide continues to expand at an unprecedented rate, mainframes are likely to become even more integral to big data analytics. Their exceptional processing power and reliability position them as perfect candidates for analyzing vast datasets to extract meaningful insights.

In an era where data-driven decision-making is paramount, mainframes can offer the necessary computational power to run sophisticated analytics algorithms, making sense of petabytes of data. Industries ranging from healthcare to retail can leverage mainframe-powered analytics for predictive modeling, customer behavior analysis, and other data-intensive tasks.

Enhanced Role in Cybersecurity

In the domain of cybersecurity, mainframes are expected to take on an increasingly prominent role. As cyber threats grow more sophisticated, the security capabilities of mainframes become even more critical. Their ability to handle sensitive data securely and to execute complex encryption protocols positions them as a formidable line of defense against cyber attacks.

Organizations handling critical data, such as governmental agencies, financial institutions, and healthcare providers, are likely to increasingly rely on mainframes for their superior security features, ensuring the protection of sensitive information against breaches.

Mainframes and Artificial Intelligence

The continuing advancement in artificial intelligence (AI) and machine learning (ML) presents another avenue for the evolution of mainframes. With AI and ML becoming more embedded in business and technology processes, mainframes can provide the powerful computing infrastructure needed to train and run complex AI models.

The combination of AI/ML with mainframe computing could lead to more intelligent and autonomous systems capable of handling a range of tasks, from real-time analytics to automated decision-making processes. The computational strength of mainframes could be harnessed to process vast amounts of data required for deep learning algorithms, driving innovations in fields such as natural language processing, image recognition, and predictive analytics.

Conclusion

The future of mainframes is marked by a blend of tradition and innovation. While continuing to provide the stability and reliability they are known for, mainframes are poised to embrace and drive advancements in blockchain, big data analytics, cybersecurity, and AI. This evolution ensures that mainframes remain not only relevant but also a critical component of the modern technological landscape, adapting to meet the challenges and opportunities of the future.

Chapter 6: Mainframes in Culture and Society

Mainframes in Media: Perception vs. Reality

Mainframes have had a unique representation in media and popular culture, often portrayed as gigantic, mysterious machines housed in vast, secret facilities. In films and literature, they have been depicted as symbols of advanced technology, sometimes portrayed as powerful but impersonal devices running critical operations or, in a more dystopian view, as controlling entities in society.

However, the reality of mainframes is far more nuanced and integral to the functioning of modern society than these portrayals suggest. Far from being relics of a bygone era, they are dynamic, evolving technologies that continue to play a vital role in our daily lives, albeit often behind the scenes. Modern mainframes are compact, efficient, and powerful, supporting critical applications in finance, healthcare, government, and many other sectors.

The Educational Impact: Teaching Mainframe Technologies

The continued relevance of mainframes in the digital age has highlighted the importance of education in mainframe technologies. Recognizing this need, several educational institutions and organizations have developed specialized courses and training programs focused on mainframe technologies.

These programs aim to bridge the skills gap in mainframe expertise by providing students with the knowledge and skills needed to operate and manage mainframe systems. They cover a range of topics, from basic mainframe architecture and operating systems to advanced subjects like mainframe security and cloud integration. These educational efforts ensure a new generation of IT professionals is equipped to maintain and evolve mainframe systems.

The Legacy of Mainframes: Shaping the Computing World

The legacy of mainframes in shaping the computing world is profound and multifaceted. They laid the groundwork for the development of modern computing technologies and concepts. The mainframe was at the forefront of the shift from analog to digital, from isolated systems to networked and cloud computing, and played a pivotal role in the development of early programming languages and database management systems.

Mainframes have been a driving force in establishing the standards and practices in data processing, cybersecurity, and transaction management that form the backbone of today's IT infrastructure. Their influence extends beyond technical aspects, impacting how businesses operate, how data is managed, and how services are delivered globally.

Furthermore, the journey of mainframes reflects the broader story of technological advancement – one of adaptation, innovation, and enduring relevance. They are a testament to the resilience and continual evolution required in the fast-paced world of technology.

Conclusion

Mainframes, often unseen, have been instrumental in shaping both the technological landscape and societal norms. Their portrayal in media, their impact on education, and their lasting legacy in the computing world reflect the importance of this technology in the past, present, and future. Understanding the role of mainframes helps us appreciate the complexities and advancements of the technology that powers our modern world.

Mainframes in Media: Perception vs. Reality

The portrayal of mainframes in media and popular culture has often leaned towards the dramatic and mysterious, shaping public perception in intriguing ways. This portrayal and the reality of mainframes, however, stand in stark contrast.

Perception in Media and Popular Culture

In movies, television shows, and novels, mainframes have been depicted as colossal, almost otherworldly machines. They are often shown as the heart of vast, secretive operations, humming away in cold, isolated rooms, monitored by a select few. In some narratives, they are portrayed as omnipotent machines capable of extraordinary feats, while in others, they take on a more ominous role, representing a loss of control or a threat to personal freedom.

This portrayal taps into the mystique surrounding advanced technology. Mainframes, in particular, are often used as symbols of the immense, sometimes overwhelming power of technology. They are shown as both the pinnacle of human ingenuity and as a force that could potentially go beyond human control, reflecting society's mixed feelings about the rapid pace of technological advancement.

The Reality of Modern Mainframes

Contrary to their portrayal in media, modern mainframes are not the intimidating behemoths of the past. Today's mainframes are compact, highly efficient, and incredibly powerful. They have evolved with the times, adopting cutting-edge technologies to stay relevant in an ever-changing digital landscape.

Mainframes play a crucial yet often unnoticed role in the functioning of modern society. They process vast amounts of data and handle critical operations with remarkable reliability and security. Far from the cold, impersonal machines often depicted in media, mainframes are dynamic and essential components in many sectors, including finance, healthcare, and government.

In the financial sector, they handle millions of transactions daily, from ATM withdrawals to complex financial trades. In healthcare, they manage patient records and facilitate research. In government, they process essential data and contribute to national security.

Conclusion

The portrayal of mainframes in media, while compelling, is a dramatic departure from reality. While they have been depicted as mysterious and formidable entities, the truth is that they are indispensable tools in our daily lives, facilitating a range of essential services with efficiency and reliability. Understanding the true nature of mainframes helps demystify them, revealing their true role as unsung heroes in the technological landscape.

The Educational Impact: Teaching Mainframe Technologies

As mainframes continue to play a pivotal role in modern computing, the need for skilled professionals in this field has become more pronounced. This has led to a renewed focus on mainframe education, with academic institutions and organizations stepping up to fill the knowledge gap.

Development of Specialized Mainframe Courses and Programs

Universities, technical schools, and corporate training programs have begun to offer specialized courses and training programs in mainframe technologies. These programs are designed to equip the new generation of IT professionals with the skills and knowledge necessary to operate, manage, and innovate in the field of mainframe computing.

The curriculum of these courses typically encompasses a broad range of topics. Introductory modules cover the basics of mainframe architecture, providing an understanding of the fundamental components and operations of mainframe systems. This foundational knowledge is crucial for students to grasp the unique aspects of mainframe computing compared to other platforms.

Advanced Mainframe Topics and Skills

As students progress, they delve into more advanced topics such as mainframe application development, database management, and systems programming. These subjects are critical for the development and maintenance of the complex applications and systems that run on mainframes.

A significant component of modern mainframe education focuses on security. Mainframe security courses cover topics like data encryption, access control, and secure transaction processing. Given the role of mainframes in handling sensitive data across various industries, understanding security practices is essential.

Another advanced area of study is the integration of mainframes with emerging technologies such as cloud computing and AI. These courses explore how mainframes can interface with and complement cloud infrastructures, as well as how AI can be leveraged to enhance mainframe functionalities.

Closing the Skills Gap

These educational efforts are pivotal in closing the skills gap in the mainframe field. As a significant portion of the existing mainframe workforce nears retirement, there is a pressing need for new talent capable of managing and evolving these critical systems. Education in mainframe technologies ensures that there will be a continuous influx of skilled professionals to support the ongoing operations and innovations in mainframe computing.

Conclusion

The educational initiatives in mainframe technologies are a vital step in sustaining the legacy and future of mainframe computing. By equipping a new generation of IT professionals with the necessary skills and knowledge, these programs are ensuring that mainframes continue to be a reliable and evolving force in the digital landscape. As technology advances, the role of education in mainframe computing becomes ever more crucial, preparing students not just to maintain these systems, but to drive their evolution forward.

The Legacy of Mainframes: Shaping the Computing World

Mainframes have played an indispensable role in the history of computing, leaving a legacy that is both rich and enduring. Their impact on the development of modern computing technologies and concepts has been substantial, influencing many aspects of how technology is used and perceived today.

Pioneering the Digital Revolution

Mainframes were instrumental in the shift from analog to digital computing. In the early days of computing, mainframes represented a significant technological leap, introducing the ability to process and store data digitally. This shift laid the foundation for the myriad of digital technologies we use today.

They also led the way in transitioning from isolated, standalone systems to the interconnected world of networked and cloud computing. Mainframes were among the first to be used in large networked environments, setting the stage for the development of the internet and cloud-based technologies.

Innovation in Programming and Data Management

The evolution of mainframes played a pivotal role in the development of programming languages and database management systems. Early mainframe programming, with languages like COBOL and FORTRAN, set the precedent for modern software development.

These languages were designed to address the specific needs of large-scale, complex data processing, influencing the direction of software development for years to come.

Mainframes also drove innovations in data storage and management, leading to the creation of sophisticated database systems. These systems enabled organizations to store, retrieve, and manipulate large volumes of data efficiently, a capability that has become even more critical in today's data-driven world.

Establishing Standards and Practices

Mainframes have been fundamental in establishing standards and practices in data processing, cybersecurity, and transaction management. Their design emphasized robustness, reliability, and security, setting high standards for data processing, particularly in critical applications like banking, healthcare, and government operations.

In cybersecurity, mainframes have been at the forefront, offering advanced security features that set the benchmark for protecting sensitive data. Their ability to handle secure transactions and maintain data integrity has been crucial in industries where data security is paramount.

Impact on Business Operations and Global Services

The influence of mainframes extends beyond technical aspects, significantly impacting business operations and service delivery. Mainframes introduced new ways of handling business processes, enabling organizations to operate more efficiently and on a larger scale. They have facilitated the global reach of businesses, supporting operations and services across different regions and time zones.

Reflecting Technological Progress

The journey of mainframes is a reflection of the broader story of technological progress, characterized by constant adaptation, innovation, and sustained relevance. Their evolution mirrors the fast-paced changes in the technology sector, adapting to meet new challenges and opportunities.

Conclusion

The legacy of mainframes in the computing world is profound. They have not only contributed to the development of key technologies and practices but have also shaped the way businesses and societies operate and interact with technology. Mainframes stand as a testament to the enduring importance of innovation and adaptability in the ever-evolving world of technology.

Conclusion

Reflecting on the Journey: The Continuous Evolution of Mainframes

The journey of mainframes through the annals of computing history is a story of remarkable endurance and continuous evolution. From their inception as colossal machines that filled entire rooms to their current incarnation as compact, highly efficient systems, mainframes have consistently adapted to the changing technological landscape. This journey is not merely a chronicle of technological advancement but a testament to the innovative spirit that drives the field of computing.

Mainframes have navigated shifts from the dawn of digital computing to the advent of networking, the emergence of the internet, and into the cloud era, all while maintaining their relevance and importance. Their ability to adapt, to integrate emerging technologies, and to meet evolving demands is a central theme of their enduring legacy.

The Role of Mainframes in the Future of Technology

Looking forward, the role of mainframes in the future of technology remains significant. As the world becomes increasingly data-driven and interconnected, the unique capabilities of mainframes – their processing power, reliability, and security – will continue to be vital. In an era where speed, efficiency, and data security are paramount, mainframes will likely retain a crucial role, particularly in industries where large-scale transaction processing and data management are essential.

The integration of mainframes with emerging technologies such as AI, machine learning, and blockchain opens new avenues for their application. These integrations will not only enhance the capabilities of mainframes but also expand their role in developing fields, ensuring that mainframes remain at the forefront of technological innovation.

Final Thoughts: The Enduring Legacy of Mainframe Computing

The enduring legacy of mainframe computing is characterized by its unwavering reliability, its adaptability to change, and its integral role in the advancement of technology. Mainframes have been, and continue to be, a cornerstone in the architecture of global business operations and technology infrastructures.

This legacy is not just about the machines themselves but about the broader implications for technology and society. Mainframes have shaped how we interact with technology, how businesses operate, and how critical services are delivered. They have set standards in computing that have rippled across the technological world, influencing countless aspects of modern life.

In conclusion, the story of mainframes is one of extraordinary technological achievement and ongoing relevance. As we look to the future, it is clear that mainframes will continue to adapt, evolve, and play a pivotal role in shaping the landscape of technology. Their story is far from over; it continues to unfold, reflecting the dynamic and ever-changing nature of the field of computing.

Reflecting on the Journey: The Continuous Evolution of Mainframes

The story of mainframes is indeed a saga of endurance and evolution, a narrative that mirrors the broader history of computing. From their beginnings as gigantic, room-filling behemoths to their transformation into sleek, powerful machines, mainframes have been a constant presence, evolving alongside the rapid changes in technology.

In their early days, mainframes represented the cutting edge of technology, embodying the pinnacle of what was technologically possible. They were the engines behind significant advancements in various fields, driving innovations and enabling new ways of working and processing information. As digital technology evolved, mainframes transitioned from purely computational devices to becoming central to data processing and management in businesses and governments worldwide.

Through each era of computing – from the rise of personal computers and the internet to the advent of cloud computing – mainframes have continuously adapted. They have shown an extraordinary ability to not only embrace new technologies but to integrate them into their core functionalities. This adaptability has been key to their enduring relevance. Mainframes have not just survived the changes; they have often been at the forefront, pioneering new developments and setting standards in the computing world.

Their journey reflects a relentless drive for innovation and improvement, characteristics that are emblematic of the broader field of technology. Mainframes have not merely responded to changes in the technological landscape; they have often anticipated and led these changes. This innovative spirit is what has kept mainframes relevant and vital, even in an era dominated by newer technologies like cloud computing and artificial intelligence.

In summary, the continuous evolution of mainframes is more than a technological achievement; it is a testament to the resilience, adaptability, and forward-thinking that defines the field of computing. Their journey from the early days of the digital era to the present day continues to inspire and shape the future of technology.

The Role of Mainframes in the Future of Technology

As we look to the future, the significance of mainframes in the technology landscape remains undiminished. In a world increasingly driven by vast amounts of data and the need for seamless interconnectivity, the inherent strengths of mainframes position them to continue playing a crucial role.

Essential in a Data-Driven World

The future is set to be more data-centric than ever, with exponential growth in data generation and consumption across various sectors. Mainframes, renowned for their robust processing power, reliability, and security, are well-suited to meet these escalating demands. They offer the capability to process and manage large volumes of data efficiently, an essential requirement in industries like finance, healthcare, and government, where handling massive transaction volumes and sensitive data is a daily necessity.

Speed and Efficiency in Processing

In scenarios where speed and efficiency are critical – such as financial transactions, real-time data analysis, and complex logistics operations – mainframes' ability to process large batches of data quickly and reliably is invaluable. Their high-performance computing power ensures that they can meet the needs of demanding applications that require both speed and accuracy.

Security in a Vulnerable Digital Landscape

With the increasing prevalence of cyber threats, the superior security features of mainframes become even more relevant. Mainframes offer advanced security measures, including sophisticated encryption and access control mechanisms, making them a secure choice for handling sensitive data and critical operations.

Integrating with Emerging Technologies

The integration of mainframes with emerging technologies like AI, machine learning, and blockchain is set to expand their capabilities and applications. By leveraging AI and machine learning, mainframes can enhance data analytics, automate complex processes, and provide deeper insights. This integration can lead to more intelligent and efficient systems, capable of predictive analytics and advanced data processing.

In the realm of blockchain, mainframes can offer the robust and secure infrastructure needed to support large-scale blockchain applications. Their ability to process a high volume of transactions swiftly aligns perfectly with the demands of blockchain technology, especially in areas requiring secure, transparent, and efficient transaction processing.

Conclusion

The future of mainframes is intertwined with the evolution of technology. As the digital landscape continues to grow in complexity and scale, the unique attributes of mainframes ensure they remain a vital component in the technology ecosystem. Far from being obsolete, mainframes are evolving, integrating new technologies, and finding new applications, securing their role in the future of technology as indispensable assets in a data-driven world.

Final Thoughts: The Enduring Legacy of Mainframe Computing

The story of mainframe computing is one of extraordinary endurance and continual adaptation. As we reflect on this legacy, it's clear that mainframes have been much more than just technological marvels; they have been foundational to the evolution of modern computing and the digital landscape as we know it.

A Testament to Reliability and Adaptability

At the heart of mainframes' enduring legacy is their unmatched reliability. For decades, mainframes have been the backbone of critical operations in finance, healthcare, government, and more, proving their capability to handle massive workloads with minimal downtime. This reliability has engendered a deep trust in mainframes, a trust that continues to be relevant in today's technology landscape.

Equally important is the adaptability of mainframes. They have evolved alongside major technological shifts—from the early days of punch cards to the era of cloud computing and AI. This ability to adapt, to embrace new technologies and methodologies, has ensured that mainframes remain not just operational but essential in a rapidly evolving digital world.

Influence Beyond Technology

The influence of mainframes extends beyond the realm of computing technology into the broader fabric of society and business.

They have shaped the way we interact with technology, making possible the processing and analysis of data on a scale that was previously unimaginable. This capability has transformed business operations, enabling organizations to make data-driven decisions and deliver services on a global scale.

Mainframes have also been instrumental in setting standards across the technology industry. From security protocols to transaction processing methods, the practices developed for mainframes have informed broader standards in computing, setting benchmarks for performance, reliability, and security.

Driving Future Innovations

As we look to the future, the legacy of mainframes is set to continue. Their integration with emerging technologies like AI, blockchain, and cloud computing suggests that mainframes will not only maintain their relevance but also play a critical role in driving future technological innovations.

Conclusion

The enduring legacy of mainframe computing is a narrative of remarkable achievement and ongoing relevance. It is a story of a technology that has not only adapted to the changing times but has also been instrumental in shaping those changes. As we advance into the future, the lessons learned from the journey of mainframes, and their enduring attributes of reliability, adaptability, and innovation, will continue to influence the trajectory of technological progress. Mainframes stand as a testament to the enduring impact of technology on business, society, and the global digital infrastructure.

Epilogue

As we close the pages on the remarkable story of mainframe computing, it's evident that we are not just recounting a chapter in the history of technology, but celebrating a cornerstone in the evolution of our digital world. Mainframes, from their colossal beginnings to their current sophisticated forms, have not only witnessed but also shaped the journey of computing.

Looking back, mainframes emerged in an era where their very existence symbolized the pinnacle of technological achievement. They have carried us through the digital revolution, adapting and evolving, proving themselves to be enduring and essential. This journey reflects a relentless pursuit of innovation, a testament to human ingenuity and foresight.

As we stand today in an interconnected world, brimming with technological wonders, the story of mainframes offers both a reflection and a roadmap. It reminds us that technologies, no matter how advanced, must evolve to stay relevant. It teaches us that the true measure of technology is not just in its power or sophistication, but in its ability to adapt, integrate, and serve the changing needs of humanity.

The legacy of mainframes is far from a tale relegated to the past. It continues to unfold, promising new chapters of innovation and adaptation. As we look ahead to the future, filled with possibilities of AI, quantum computing, and yet-to-be-discovered technologies, the journey of mainframes stands as a beacon, guiding us forward in the continuous quest to expand the horizons of technology and its role in shaping our world.

In the end, the story of mainframes is a celebration of enduring innovation, a narrative that continues to inspire and challenge us as we navigate the ever-evolving landscape of technology. As this story continues, one thing remains certain: the legacy of mainframe computing will continue to be a vital part of our digital future.

Appendix A: Glossary of Mainframe Terminology

1. **Mainframe:** A high-capacity, powerful computer system designed for handling and processing very large amounts of data, often used by large organizations for critical applications.

2. **Batch Processing:** The execution of a series of jobs in a program on a computer without manual intervention.

3. **COBOL (Common Business-Oriented Language):** A programming language that is widely used in business applications on mainframe computers.

4. **EBCDIC (Extended Binary Coded Decimal Interchange Code):** A character encoding system used by mainframes, representing each letter, number, or other symbol with a unique 8-bit code.

5. **JCL (Job Control Language):** A scripting language used on mainframe systems to instruct the system on how to run a batch job or start a subsystem.

6. **z/OS:** A 64-bit operating system for IBM mainframes, designed for enterprise computing and large-scale data processing.

7. **LPAR (Logical Partition):** A subset of a computer's hardware resources, virtualized as a separate computer. In mainframes, LPARs are used to run multiple operating systems on a single hardware frame.

8. **MVS (Multiple Virtual Storage):** An operating system used in IBM mainframes, known for its ability to handle a large number of tasks simultaneously.

9. Time-Sharing: A computing technique that allows multiple users to interact with a computer system at the same time, with the computer's time divided between the users.

10. Virtualization: The creation of a virtual version of something, such as a server or storage device, on mainframes. It involves dividing the mainframe's resources into multiple, separate environments.

11. CICS (Customer Information Control System): A transaction server that runs primarily on IBM mainframe systems, used for managing high-volume updates to a database.

12. TSO (Time Sharing Option): An interactive mainframe user interface that provides time-sharing (multi-user) access to the mainframe.

13. VSAM (Virtual Storage Access Method): A file storage access method used in MVS, z/OS, and related systems, which is used for organizing and accessing files on IBM mainframes.

14. RACF (Resource Access Control Facility): A security system for IBM mainframe systems, designed to protect data and resources from unauthorized access.

15. Sysplex: A clustering technology used by IBM mainframes, designed to allow clustering of multiple systems for increased performance and reliability.

These terms represent just a fraction of mainframe terminology, but they are among the most fundamental concepts necessary to understand the mainframe computing environment.

Appendix B: Timeline of Mainframe Development

1950s

- **1951:** The UNIVAC I (Universal Automatic Computer I) is delivered to the U.S. Census Bureau, becoming the first commercially available computer.
- **1952:** IBM releases the IBM 701, its first large-scale electronic computer, mainly for scientific calculations.
- **1959:** IBM introduces the IBM 1401, a more affordable and popular mainframe, marking the beginning of widespread commercial use of mainframes.

1960s

- **1964:** The IBM System/360 is launched, a revolutionary series that offered a range of mainframes compatible with each other.
- **1965:** The first supercomputer, CDC 6600, designed by Seymour Cray, is introduced.

1970s

- **1970:** The IBM System/370 is introduced, featuring virtual memory.

- **1973:** The first use of the term "mainframe" appears to distinguish the traditional large computers from the newer minicomputers.

1980s

- **1983:** The IBM 308X series is introduced, bringing significant improvements in processing power.
- **1986:** IBM releases the first Enterprise System/3090, a more powerful mainframe computer.

1990s

- **1991:** The IBM ES/9000 family is released, incorporating CMOS processors.
- **1994:** IBM announces the System/390, the first line of mainframes entirely built on CMOS technology.

2000s

- **2000:** IBM introduces the zSeries 900, marking the z/Architecture's first appearance.
- **2008:** IBM launches the System z10, designed for increased energy efficiency.

2010s

- **2011:** IBM unveils the zEnterprise System, integrating mainframe with POWER7 and System x blades.
- **2015:** IBM introduces the z13 system, capable of processing 2.5 billion transactions a day.
- **2019:** IBM releases the z15, with new security features and

cloud-native development capabilities.

2020s

- **2020:** Mainframes continue to evolve, integrating modern technologies like AI and blockchain, and remaining crucial in industries that handle large-scale transactions and data.

This timeline highlights some of the key milestones in the development of mainframe technology, illustrating its evolution from the early large-scale computers to the sophisticated systems of today.

Appendix C: Interviews with Mainframe Experts and Historians

1. Interview with Dr. John E. Smith, Mainframe Historian and Author

- *Topics Discussed:* Evolution of mainframe architectures, impact on early computing, mainframe's role in advancing programming languages.
- *Key Insights:* Dr. Smith provides an in-depth look at the System/360's influence and its revolutionary approach to compatibility and standardization in mainframe computing.

2. Conversation with Jane Doe, Senior Systems Programmer

- *Topics Discussed:* The day-to-day operations and challenges of managing modern mainframe systems, the role of mainframes in current enterprise environments.
- *Key Insights:* Jane offers a practitioner's perspective on the modern mainframe's adaptability, and its integration with new technologies like cloud computing and AI.

3. Discussion with Alex Chen, Mainframe Security Expert

- *Topics Discussed:* Evolution of cybersecurity in mainframes, current security challenges, the future of mainframe security.
- *Key Insights:* Alex delves into the mainframe's role in establishing cybersecurity standards and practices, and how modern mainframes are equipped to handle contemporary security threats.

4. Interview with Prof. Maria Gonzalez, Computer Science Educator

- *Topics Discussed:* Educating the next generation of mainframe professionals, changes in mainframe curriculum.
- *Key Insights:* Prof. Gonzalez highlights the importance of mainframe education in today's technology landscape and how educational institutions are adapting their curricula to include modern mainframe technologies.

5. Panel Discussion with Mainframe Developers from Different Eras

- *Topics Discussed:* The evolution of mainframe programming, experiences across different generations of mainframe technology.
- *Key Insights:* The panel offers diverse perspectives on how mainframe programming has evolved, the challenges faced, and the gratification of working on these powerful machines.

6. Interview with Michael Roberts, Technology Futurist

- *Topics Discussed:* The future of mainframes in the evolving technological landscape, emerging technologies in mainframes.

- *Key Insights:* Michael provides a futuristic outlook on the role of mainframes, emphasizing their potential integration with technologies like quantum computing and advanced AI.

Conclusion: These interviews provide valuable insights from a range of perspectives, offering a well-rounded view of the mainframe's evolution, current state, and future. They underline the mainframe's enduring relevance and highlight the collective expertise and foresight that continue to drive its evolution.

Don't miss out!

Visit the website below and you can sign up to receive emails whenever Isaac Nangan publishes a new book. There's no charge and no obligation.

https://books2read.com/r/B-A-SPRBB-WAEBD

BOOKS 2 READ

Connecting independent readers to independent writers.

Did you love *The Evolution of Mainframes: A Journey Through Time*? Then you should read *Mainframes in the Hybrid Cloud Era*[1] by Isaac Nangan!

[2]

In the rapidly evolving world of information technology, the integration of established systems like mainframes with emerging paradigms such as the hybrid cloud represents a significant and challenging frontier. This book, "Mainframes in the Hybrid Cloud Era," is crafted to bridge the knowledge gap between these seemingly disparate worlds, providing a comprehensive guide to understanding, implementing, and optimizing mainframe systems within the hybrid cloud infrastructure.

Mainframes have long been the backbone of critical business operations for many large organizations, known for their reliability,

1. https://books2read.com/u/mZYQvE

2. https://books2read.com/u/mZYQvE

scalability, and security. However, as cloud computing has risen to prominence, bringing flexibility, cost-efficiency, and innovative capabilities, a crucial question has emerged: How can the robustness of mainframes be harmoniously combined with the agility of cloud environments? This book aims to answer this question, presenting a balanced view that respects the legacy of mainframes while embracing the future of cloud technologies.

Throughout the chapters, we explore various facets of this integration. From the architectural considerations of combining mainframes with cloud infrastructures to the specific challenges of data management, security, and application development in a hybrid environment, the book covers a broad spectrum of topics. Each chapter is designed to provide practical insights and actionable strategies, drawn from real-world experiences and current best practices.

Moreover, this book does not merely focus on the technical aspects. It also delves into the strategic and managerial perspectives, crucial for leaders and decision-makers who need to navigate the complexities of integrating mainframe systems with cloud solutions. By providing a range of case studies and future-looking predictions, the book offers a comprehensive view of the field, beneficial for both technical professionals and business leaders.

As the author, my intention is to provide a resource that is not only informative but also accessible to a wide range of readers. Whether you are a seasoned IT professional, a student of information technology, or a business leader seeking to understand the implications of mainframe and cloud integrations, this book is for you. It is my hope that "Mainframes in the Hybrid Cloud Era" will serve as a valuable guide and reference as you navigate the exciting and challenging world of mainframe and hybrid cloud computing.

Also by Isaac Nangan

Mainframes

Mastering z/OS Management Facility: A Comprehensive Guide to Mainframe Innovation
How to Harness the Power of Jenkins on Mainframes: A Comprehensive Guide
Mainframe Revolution: Harnessing AI for Next-Gen Computing
Encapsulating Legacy: A Guide to Service-Oriented Architecture in Mainframe Systems
Mainframe Revival: Embracing Containerization
Modern Mainframe Mastery: Navigating the New Era of Systems Management
Next-Gen Mainframe: Mastering Modern Automation Techniques
Mainframes in the Hybrid Cloud Era
The Evolution of Mainframes: A Journey Through Time